between
black
& white

short poems
by
michael r guerin

Other Titles by Michael R. Guerin

POETRY:
  Ghosts, Flames & Ashes
  world thru a window
  mind & machine
  between black & white
  still life
  Found & Lost
  beneath the waves
  Flowers for Rumi
  Ocean Rain
  Vespers

FICTION:
  The Otherside

ORACLE DECKS & GUIDEBOOKS:
  Nature Speaks: A Lenormand Deck & Guidebook
  Vincent Speaks: A Healing Oracle Deck & Guidebook

ISBN: 978-0-578-41524-6
Imprint: Independently published

Table of Contents

i. red

ii. yellow

iii. blue

"What is the art of living? Where there is division in us psychologically there must be conflict, and therefore disorder. As long as there is disorder, trying to find order is still disorder."

– J Krishnamurti

i.

red

"What would life be
if we had no courage
to attempt anything?"

~ Vincent

mirage

beneath a field of wine
speckled with fire
the air cool and dry, weightless —
i swim in a sea of delights
intoxicated by life.
how your skin holds the setting sun's flame
and raven hair trails to cascade
like vines down the side of your face.
in midnight my spirit burns skyward
climbing heaven's stair
through layers of rarefied air
to meet you there.

it passes you by

beneath wrought iron lamps
the red brick street glistens
from a cool drizzle.

with each passing step
my warm and familiar
bar stool

slowly recedes
into a yellowed past
i can no longer imagine.

somewhere up ahead
her black front door
stands secured
against all strangers

and neatly hung
with a brass number plate
i was never given
to answer.

still shivered

there's never one reason for leaving
(though mistaken heads nod
in approval at fables offered up
as truth) for crows will fly
in any direction they choose
(just ask van gogh)...
and the shivered tenor
of a voice singing the blues
so soulfully rendered
in a moment unplugged
which drifts through the pines
as his song unwinds
is executed for its own particular sake.

(for kurt cobain)

an untamed "i"

at home in the dark
i am bated breath
and base desire,
or the haunting notes
of an unsung aria
echoing into night
as holy fire.

i am that which is wounded
yet forever burns
in the magic
of unspoken words
(felt as the barest whisper
from my touch) —

a whirling rush
of shadow
and light which dances
beyond ecstasy
or shame,
always new
and eternally untamed.

heavy with paint

in dreams i'm holding
the brush again,
my index finger pointed
at bristles heavy with paint.

from across the room
i can barely make out
her silhouette
beneath a flimsy sheet,

and enthralled
by the rise and fall
of her chest
with each passing breath

my trembling hand
dares transpose
her indescribable beauty,
stroke by stroke.

and then i wake —
left with only
a barren canvas unable
to hold her shape.

a fan of summer

at the risk of sounding cliche
life flowed differently back then...

on hot summer days windows
would be flung open wide

inviting any stray breeze
to blow through rusted screens.

and carried on hot air
the sounds of children

playing outdoors, their screams
of anger or delight

mingled with bird calls
and barking dogs

along with the gentle rustle
of green leaves dancing

float in with each gust of wind.
but that was before cable tv

or central ac when rotary
fans wobbled atop tables

rhythmically spraying blasts
of stale air from side to side

into faces eager for any relief
while our dads chain-

smoked and played pinochle
as decks got shuffled

and cards were dealt
with our moms out of earshot,

happily seated in floral living
rooms spinning yarns

about family dramas
while taking their turns

to spill the tea amid bursts
of wild laughter

like so many passes
from that old rotary fan.

still falling

still falling —
like a withered maple leaf
from the tree outside your window
or the first few flakes of snow
on a cold december evening
or the weight of salty tears
when i left you like a stranger
and the time we stood
like statues for hours
in the rain.

it's taken
too long to realize
that there's nothing left to gain...
and now the better part of me
dares dream the sweetest
life with you, together
and still falling —
calling out
your name.

all a twitter

anger in any form is anger,
naked and pure.
righteous indignation is never righteous.
indignation is nothing more
than anger poorly
dressed in finer clothes.
and when a wave of anger rises
the masses smell blood,
demanding heads and vengeance
which drowns out calmer voices
beneath its roiling red tide.
socially speaking
we're not very sociable,
except when driven mad with rage
as we wage another war
communally justified.

(for jimmy kimmel)

down route 113

i still remember drives down
route 113 laying on the back
seat staring up through
a side window with the sky
broken every now and again
as power lines passed by.
we drove in silence
to a nameless hospital
where words like "cancer"
and "chemo" didn't mean much
to a young boy's mind
and once there i sat quiet
and still in an antiseptic hall
where people dressed in white
would pass by and remark
on how smart i looked
or how well i behaved
while i waited for my mémère
to emerge from some mysterious
place. finally we'd return
to her home to be greeted
with the welcoming smell
of homemade chicken soup
and sitting at the kitchen table
i heard her say "he's too
young to see me like this"
and my mom replied

"it will make him a good
man, ma" but lost in a game
of cards or steaming bowls
of chicken soup
i had no way of knowing
that one cold december
morning and not long
enough from then
in the barest blink
of an eye that world
would forever
be erased.

a betrayal

in a millisecond
you can feel it ring true
that knowing without knowing
in your gut or in your bones
which communicates more
than a million words ever could
about the state of a soul
in the barest glance of her clear blue
eyes even before a single tear
forms and eventually streaks
earthwards under the weight of her world
gliding down a porcelain cheek
you were once given for kisses
or the tremor in a voice about to break
into tiny shards of shattered glass
just before she asks
you to leave and never come back
and how your face
flush with shame betrays
you in ways your
words never would.

open suitcase

it's too easy to leave
one who's already lost...

but when love's the rage
and nothing else matters

and days melt into endless days
with betrayals exchanged
despite any cost,

then how or when
can a heart ever decide

to cleave those final few ties
which forever blind

and with a pair
of borrowed wings
finally take to flight?

once upon a when

these feet once filled with rage
prowled familiar streets and lanes
in my dreams, in my drunken
hours desperate for love's embrace

or a single touch given
with meaning and deeply felt
against another solitary night.

was it madness that led to endless
flights into golden fields
armed with brush and paint
eager to transform the landscapes

of my world, of my dreams
while you slept so peacefully
and exquisitely out of reach?

(for vincent)

ii.

yellow

"I don't know anything
with certainty, but seeing the stars
makes me dream."

~ Vincent

dreaming in yellow

when passion runs deep
what bubbles to the surface?

behind each facade a face
like any other in disguise.

to meet you i suppose
from postcards left behind.

beneath each starry sky
a soul can rattle its cage.

dried strokes on the page
just a moment in time.

an august afternoon

in the distance a mower
drones its low rumble.
from my bedroom window
all backyards seem vain.

a murder of crows land
on my neighbor's lawn
pecking at unseen bugs
for their daily bread.

beneath this midday glare
all thoughts run together
bleached white
by an unrelenting dread.

in the distance gray clouds
gather on the horizon
while i sit here quietly
and pray for rain.

on a melancholy angle

early morning rays break the horizon
with earnest anticipation
of what might come to pass,

while soft and subtle colors
are bleached white when drenched
in the harsh glare of midday light.

but late afternoon summer sunshine
hangs reverently in warm air
slanting sweetly through shivering
silver-green leaves
of towering poplar and beech
on a melancholy angle.

(for emily dickinson)

late afternoon

sitting beneath a tangle
of branches and grateful
for their shade

a bird whose name
i'll never know
rested on a limb.

and looking down
for some response,sang
its song of life,

or perhaps just a call
for other birds to perch
nearby just so

while cool autumn breezes
kissed tall grasses
ready for a mowing.

fireflies

as a little boy i'd wait
for summer evening skies
to be filled with fireflies
and gazed in fascination
as their tails lit up the night.
and running barefoot on cool grass
would catch them in my hands,
and lucky enough to find one in my grasp
would peek between gently closed
fingers to see its pale glow
shine on innocent palms
yet to cause harm
in this fragile world
we reluctantly
call home.

colors dance

yellow leaves
skate past
the patio door,

their desiccated
shapes fragile
and torn.

perhaps this year
i'll let
november breezes

rake them away
from my buckwheat
lawn.

a note from skógafoss

words fail us at nearly every turn.
wrapped in a web of ideas
about how things work
and pushed to justify inherited beliefs
which form the ground of our understanding
is it any wonder that faced
with unadorned reality
there's nothing left to say —
and what would you offer anyway

to a waterfall that has no need
for schemes as pure water pours
from a mountain which formed
when no one was around,
and how it will stand strong
rooted in this place majestic and sure
stretching out into a timeless
count of tomorrows long
after our bones returned to dust.

i lied

joanie's "diamonds and rust"
echoes in my earbuds
for the seventeenth time

as i sip an ice-cold beer
and remember
the day you left.

while the station's platform
bustled with travelers
bound for nowhere

you bit your lower lip
and, eyes locked on mine,
asked if i'd be alright.

without missing a beat
i lied, november
gusts tousling your hair,

my frozen smile betraying
nothing before
a last kiss goodbye.

in flux

outside my window
a cold gale
rattles
wooden shutters.

a dog's howl echoes
over black
and white streets
as the lights flicker.

a blank sheet
of yellow paper torn
with razor-blade
precision

mocks my attempts
to unlock
a single thought
worth sharing.

goodbye, my indigo

indigo fades into pale yellow
moment by moment,
degree by slightest degree —
and beneath an empty firmament
devoid of dreams
perhaps you'll make your way
through another hollow day
wondering what it all
might mean.

iii.

blue

"I often think that the night
is more alive and more richly
colored than the day."

~ Vincent

bittersweet and blue

without a single word
your clear brown eyes
reach out across this distance

and cut me to the bone
and lay my falsehoods bare
in ways bittersweet and blue

which leaves my spirit empty
and hungry
to hold some truth.

i doubt if you remember
such a slivered slice
of space or time and i wonder

what you're doing
and how your life has been
in the silent traces of an hour

filled with recollections
bold and blue
as my thoughts melt into you.

for all the life

we see what we want to see
at a traffic light
or by the beach
or cruising eighty miles an hour
down a dusty highway
in the middle of nowhere
with nowhere to go.

and it comes as no surprise
that each comparison
pulls us further and further
from any hope of truth
and each judgment about the world
just another nail
in our future coffin.

you ask what i'm thinking
while the tv drones on about some war
or toxic waste between commercials
for beer and tooth paste
but not in a million years
do i dare share
thoughts which perpetually
pass through this mind of mine.

stray from the track trodden
down by centuries of blind faith

and be labeled —
mercilessly.

but for a sensitive soul
your sensible world
seems more and more senseless
each passing hour
each passing day
and for all the life left in me
i can't call your sanity sane.

a letter

your words have finally reached me
from out of the cold
and out from the past
and it's more than i could
have hoped for and more
than i ever knew
and as the years melt away
between us i'm able to see at last
how nothing that's true
ever passes for a heart
that's willing to ask.

last night

her parting words hang heavy
in the air as the car door
slams shut. through its open window
you watch as she strides
up a gravel path to her front porch
lit by two yellow bulbs buzzing
with a cloud of moths and mosquitoes.
she fishes a key from her purse
and without a pause or glance
back in your direction unlocks
the door and slips inside
her darkened home. behind
drawn curtains the muted glow
of a lamp greets the night
and from memory you picture
those slow barefooted steps
towards a back bedroom
as her dress slides
off silken shoulders
and comes to rest
on the cold
wooden floor.

the tolling bell

wrapped in grief's embrace
never sweetly felt
what lingers deep inside
to rattle a chest cold as ice

while reason wanders past?
and lost in darkness
blacker than night
without a path to guide,

how can a soul
truly rent apart
ever find its weary
way back?

(triptych on grief, part i)

(for fanny brawne)

the colors that i seek

shall any aspire to measure
the beat of a broken heart
or dare weigh such depth of feeling
between two rendered souls?

and yet as so often happens
far removed by time or space
the masses shoot dull arrows
from a worldview hung with rags

as if dead words might matter
to echo love's hidden truth
revealed thru spirit's passing
along its hallowed path.

(triptych of grief, part ii)

it comes like ice

behind your tears which flow
and those stuck frozen as ice
unshed upon a cheek,
unbled upon a soul duly rent

is a feeling felt with reason
unable to gain release
of a thought held fast as fact
of what won't come to pass

and an ending of a dream
you'd rather not let go, or surrender —
like the fatal blossom's kiss
you cannot unremember.

(triptych of grief, part iii)

as it echoes

i'm not naive enough
to believe
that a well said word
if properly heard
makes a damn bit of difference

in the end.
but as a deeply felt note
can split the night
the only choice left
is to cast your voice

over the waves
and let it echo into void
for its own sake
even if no one ever bothers
to stop or listen.

no denial

maybe it's strange how life
worked out this way, like
how i can't deny your face
burned into my brain
with razor sharp precision.

or how most starry nights
lying atop a tiled roof
wrapped in anonymity
i watched each exhale
trail upwards as warm vapor

only to disappear into cool air
as the next october breeze
blew past my best laid plans.
and now, how most days
it's a fight to keep

focused on the task at hand
without seeing your face
burned into this brain
white hot like a brand
on each page of my memory.

a late october night

beneath yellow streetlamps
damp oak leaves glisten,
stuck on pavement
like confetti.

summer parties long over,
we walk in elemental silence
where everything worth saying
hangs by a thread.

each step pulls us further
from your empty home
shuttered against
the impending cold.

up ahead a pickup truck
speeds down the narrow lane
with high beams
blinding both our faces.

my exhaled breath
hangs mid-air,
then slowly dissolves
into night.

dying embers

a cold drizzle
sheets bare branches
hung like copper wire
and devoid of crows.

three straight days of rain
have transformed
my lawn
into an impenetrable bog.

with a wrought iron poker
i rake gray ashes
hoping to catch
the last few logs.

satisfied, i sit
on the hearth and sip
my coffee
as embers glow.

"Freedom and love go together. Love is not a reaction. If I love you because you love me, that is mere trade, a thing to be bought in the market; it is not love. **To love is not to ask anything in return, not even to feel that you are giving something** - and it is only such love that can know freedom."

— J. Krishnamurti

Acknowledgments

There are probably a lot of reasons why someone feels compelled to create, whether it's writing a song, painting on canvas, telling a story or crafting a poem. To be entirely honest with you after my first book of poetry was published I thought I was "finished." That I had nothing more to "say," so to speak. Or share. Clearly that wasn't the case.

I don't know what will come next, if anything (who does?). To echo the words of dear Vincent...

> "I must continue to follow the path I take now. If I do nothing, if I study nothing, if I cease searching, then, woe is me, I am lost. That is how I look at it – keep going, keep going come what may."

Of course, the path I follow is not without some very dear traveling companions. There are simply too many people to thank who have helped me along the way, so this time I'll focus on only two...

First and foremost my wife and best friend of nearly twenty years, Rumpa. Every day with her feels as fresh and new as the first, and life with her has been anything but boring.

Then there's my dear friend ("brother") Mark Shepard

who continues to cheer me on even when I sometimes consider this enterprise (i.e. writing poetry) to be nothing more than a fool's errand. But as the old adage goes ("if a tree falls in the woods and no one is there to hear it, does it make a sound?") the fact remains that whether or not anyone experiences your artistic endeavors really doesn't matter in the end. Just cast your "voice" out across the endless waters, for its own sake.

Ultimately, I believe we are here to "create," come what may. And the simple fact of the matter is that the most important "work of art" we're here to work on is our very own life. In this respect, we are both artist and work of art. What's more, every act of creation is an expression of energy which helps to transform this world (even if it seems a fool's errand), whether or not anyone ever ultimately interacts with or appreciates the "things" which we create.

Finally, a heart-felt thank you to you for getting a copy of this book and choosing to spend some precious time in these pages. Hopefully something resonated with you, and if not then please accept my sincere apology.

Cover design by:
Angie @ pro_ebookcovers

About Michael R Guerin

Michael R. Guerin is a veteran of the U.S. Air Force, a former Catholic religious community postulant and the founder of Success Marketing, a web design firm. He has a Master's Degree in Philosophy from Fordham University, is the author of eight books of poetry (available on amazon.com), a Lenormand Deck & Guidebook and the creator of a van Gogh inspired oracle deck (available on etsy.com). Since 2008 he has set up, redesigned or fixed more than six hundred websites, many for holistic health practitioners. He recently completed his first novel, THE OTHERSIDE, which is the first of a planned four book series titled "The Wanderer." The series is a past-life recollection which weaves together four different historical timelines and focuses on love, loss, mission and redemption. He currently lives in the greater Orlando area with his wife and family.

www.ingramcontent.com/pod-product-compliance
Lightning Source LLC
Chambersburg PA
CBHW061159040426
42445CB00013B/1744